How to Spot One of Us

How to Spot One of Us

Poems

Janet R. Kirchheimer

2007 • 5768
CLAL–The National Jewish Center for Learning and Leadership

How to Spot One of Us
Poems
Janet R. Kirchheimer

Copyright © 2007 by CLAL–The National Jewish Center
for Learning and Leadership

CLAL–The National Jewish Center
for Learning and Leadership
440 Park Avenue South, 4th floor
New York, NY 10016
www.clal.org

Author Photo: Roslyn Dickens

Cover design: Janet R. Kirchheimer and Bill Kobasz /
Reliable Design Studios

Book design: Aliza J. Kaplan and Janet R. Kirchheimer

Manufactured in the United States of America

ISBN 13: 978-0-9633329-8-1

CONTENTS

Foreword by Rabbi Irwin Kula   ix
Introduction by Rabbi Irving "Yitz" Greenberg   xi

I

At the Picture Window	3
Things My Father Won't Do	4
Family Gathering	5
Picnic	6
Boundaries	7
Echoes	8
How I Knew and When	9
Regarding Niederstetten, Shabbos Morning, March 25, 1933	11
Summer Afternoon, 1934	13
Keeping Watch, 1936	14
Traces	15
Berlin to Hamburg, Summer, 1938	16
Town Hall	17
Breaking Laws	18
Lines	20
If You Were Lucky	21
Testing Ground	22
A Good Job	23
A Simple Gesture	25
String	26
Shopping in Dachau	27
One Night	28
Hand-me-down Clothing	29
Release from Dachau	30
Getting a Visa	31
My Father's Sister	32
Josef	33

II

Setting Out 37

House of Cards 38

Greenhorn 39

Western Union 40

The Photograph in My Hand 41

Retelling 42

The Way to a Visa 43

My Mother's Sister, Resi 44

This Is How My Opa Strauss Died 46

The American Branch of the Family 48

Comforts 49

Brothers 51

Birthday Wishes 52

Opa Kirchheimer 53

Tell Me, Josef 54

Found: Four Postcards to a Friend
    Before Deportation to Auschwitz 55

Thursday Afternoon at the Joods Historisch
    Museum, Amsterdam 57

Passages 58

In Oma Kirchheimer's Hand 59

Cost of Life, America, 1944 60

Holocaust Victim Assets Litigation Initial Questionnaire 61

It Has Been Reported 62

Justice 63

III

Missing	67
If	68
How to Spot One of Us	69
Lunchtime	70
At the Butcher's	71
Jury Duty	72
On My Way to Work	73
Waiting	74
Grand Central Station	75
Rooms on the Left, Rooms on the Right	76
Inside a Cattle Car	77
The Promised Land	78
Daughter of Holocaust Survivors	79
Learning to Swim	80
Family History	81
Imprints	82
Ruth Is My Middle Name	83
Rituals	84
What Fathers Tell Sons	85
Some of the Things I Wonder	86
Sisters	87
A Daughter Dreams	88
Sweet Dreams	89

IV

Learning a New Language 93
Oma Kirchheimer 94
Sound Barrier 95
Ashes 96
Possessions 97
Maastricht, January, 2007 98
Dogs 99
The Bird Feeder 100
Thinning Out the Carrots 102
Planting 103

Notes 105
Acknowledgments 110
About the Author 113
About CLAL 114

FOREWORD

One of the first poems Janet R. Kirchheimer shared with me contained disarmingly few lines describing the simple act of eating which forever changed my experience of walking into a pizza parlor. This is the power of her poetry. Nothing ordinary—whether a photograph, a picnic at the beach, a yearly doctor's check-up, a chaise lounge, a birthday cake, feeding the birds, or shoveling snow, to list just a very few of the images in these pages—is ever the same after one has read her evocative work, and this is as it should be after the Holocaust. A daughter of survivors, she has taken in the silences, nightmares, stories, fragments, and memories of her parents and, in return, with utter honesty, compassion, artistry, and precision gives us a sacred glimpse (all we can ever have) of how such pain and suffering transform the way one imagines, sees, hears, feels, smells, and tastes the world. There is pain, rage, and awe, and yet when one finishes reading these poems one concludes that better an unreasonable love than the deadly, deadening hatred that curdles life.

Theodor Adorno wrote that poetry after the Holocaust would be a barbaric act. Janet R. Kirchheimer proves in *How to Spot One of Us* that poetry after the Holocaust can be a holy act, inviting us to see that the mystery and inscrutability of evil carry within them a response, not of hatred but of an ever-constant love, which triumphs over evil in the only way it can for finite human beings—in the details of the love between a husband and wife, parents and daughter, a family and its past. Janet R. Kirchheimer has taken a particular Jewish event—the Holocaust—a particular family's experiences, and the personal and intimate details of particular people in particular places at particular moments and has aspired to a universal revelation of a new sense of reality, knowing full well that the Holocaust was the new reality. There is no easy catharsis here and yet as we read these poems and experience the intimacy of tragedy, loss, anguish, and despair we are invited with fierce grace to preserve our humanity and faith.

As President of CLAL–The National Jewish Center for Learning and Leadership, I am particularly grateful and moved that we have the privilege of publishing this haunting collection. May it penetrate your heart, pierce your soul, and inspire you to remember.

Rabbi Irwin Kula

INTRODUCTION

Even if all the trees were turned into quills and the oceans of the
world into ink, one could not tell all the pain, all the suffering, all
the stories of the Shoah. It is part of the cruel victory of the Nazis
that inevitably many lives will be swallowed up in the final abyss of
oblivion. But here comes Janet R. Kirchheimer's little miracle of a
book with a victory over forgetfulness. It presents itself as poetry,
but no matter; it is really Scriptural narrative. The book holds up
for our observation the story of her mother, Margot, who was one
of four girls (out of 104) in the Israelitisch Meisjes Weeshuis
orphanage in Amsterdam who survived, and of her father, Bule
Kirchheimer (that's what his little brother, Josef, used to call him
when they were kids; Josef never grew up to call him Julius). The
author holds us in her grasp and, scene by scene, story by story,
fellow sufferer by fellow sufferer, the book makes us see what
happened.

Hold this book reverently. It is a Kaddish for the dead Oma and
Opa and Ruth and Josef Kirchheimer and the boys' choir of the
Levetzowstrasse shul; and for her maternal grandmother, Oma
Strauss, who bought her mother red Mary Jane shoes on the way
home from the American Consulate; and for the *shochet*, Gerson
Rosenthal, and for the man who froze to death in Dachau one
night; and for the kapo who told Julius to keep his mouth shut
so when the SS aim the fire hoses at him he won't swallow water
and choke; and for the man who went crazy in the barracks and ...
and ... and....

As we read, we realize another remarkable truth. The silent,
motionless vibration of memory sets off a powerful, ever-present
resonance in our mind. Like the author's, our consciousness and
heart will be forever haunted—reverberating ceaselessly. The poems
come to us deceptively mild, half apologetic, sweetly, modestly self-

abnegating. But they are powerfully disguised; like fearsome new flesh-eating viruses, they reproduce and devour everything in their path. Only, when they burrow into us they inject compassion, not death. Infected, we are flushed not with fever but with warm and merciful feelings.

These poems are relentless—summoning up the events, echoing the footfalls of the tortured wayfarers on the road of agony; then invading our silences, penetrating our dreams, shaping our perceptions of other experiences. Here you will learn why some days you can't eat pizza (it's the ovens) and why taking a number at the butcher jeopardizes your sanity. And we discover that the stories will be modulated and transferred in the form of emotional kinetic energy into all the relationships and interactions in our lives. Reading, we are transformed. And we are better persons for it.

Isaiah said of Holy Writ (55:10-11): "For as the rain and snow come down from the heavens and will not return there but will water the earth and make it bring forth and blossom, yielding seed for the sower and bread to the eater, so My word that issues from My mouth shall not return to Me empty-handed but will accomplish what I desired and achieve what I sent it to do."

We can say of this book: As the rain and snow come down from the heavens and will not return there but will water the earth and make it bring forth and blossom ... so shall the words written in this book not return empty-handed but will infuse the mind of every reader, giving life to the dead and compassion to the living.

Rabbi Irving "Yitz" Greenberg
Chairman Emeritus
United States Holocaust Memorial Council

To My Family, Who Has Taught Me

Love is stronger than death.

—Song of Songs 8:6

I

At the Picture Window

The snow falls
and I watch my father
shovel the driveway
and the more he shovels
the more snow
falls and he
can't clear away
the snow and I
can't stop the snow
from turning to ashes
before it falls to the ground.

Things My Father Won't Do

wear striped clothing
go to the doctor
tell me his dreams
live in a house surrounded by a fence

Family Gathering

My father watches war documentaries, footage of people
arriving for the selections at Auschwitz.
I think he hopes to see his family.

My mother begins to cry.
My brother walks out.
I sit.

Picnic

Sunday mornings during the summer,
my parents would pack up our blue Ford
and we'd head to the beach,
my brother and I in the back seat, the trunk filled
with bathing suits, chairs, and an aluminum ice chest.

We'd eat in the same pavilion,
at the same wooden picnic table.
My mother would cover the table, put out
peanut-butter-and-jelly or baloney sandwiches,
some flavor of Kool-Aid, and fruit for dessert.

A large Italian family sat at the next table.
Grandmothers, dressed all in black, dished
food from large pots.
People were always coming to their table.
Relatives, I'd tell myself.

Aunts and uncles yelled at the kids
to sit at the table, the kids my age,
cousins, playing, fighting, screaming,
and I'd watch them from our table,
that big family, mine so small.

Boundaries

When we would visit Fred and Carola Stein,
my father and Fred would stand off to the side
of the dining room and talk quietly.

When I walked in, they would stop speaking.
They didn't want me to hear, didn't want me to know.

I wanted to know but kept walking.

Echoes

"When I went away to trade school in Berlin,"
my father tells me, "I would go to the Levetzowstrasse shul.
A boys' choir sang every Shabbos.
Even from the street, I could hear the singing."

I ask what it sounded like, and he tells me,
"It was like nothing you've ever heard, so beautiful
you wouldn't believe it."

I ask what happened to the shul.
He tells me it was turned into a deportation center.
I don't ask any more questions.

How I Knew and When

Age 8 – My father hangs upside down on a pipe that was part of a fence
that separated our street from the next. All of his change
falls from his pockets. He looks so young.

Age 15 – "There were one hundred and four girls
in the Israelitisch Meisjes Weeshuis orphanage in Amsterdam.
Four survived," my mother says.
"I remember Juffrouw Frank, the headmistress. She made us
drink cod-liver oil each morning. She said it was healthy for us."

Age 17 – My father tells me his father and sister Ruth got out
of Germany and went to Rotterdam. They were supposed to
leave on May 11, 1940, for America. The Nazis invaded on May 10.

Age 21 – My mother tells me Tante Amalia told her
that on the Queen Elizabeth to America in 1947, after she
and Onkel David were released from an internment camp
on the Isle of Man, she was so hungry she ate twelve rolls
each day at breakfast. She said it was the best time she ever had.

Age 24 – My father tells me, "Otto Reis got out of Germany
in 1941. He took a train to Moscow, the Trans-Siberian railroad to
Vladivostok, a boat to Shanghai, a boat to Yokohama, a boat to
San Francisco, and a bus to Philadelphia, his wife and three sons
staying behind. Carola Stein signed affidavits for them, but
the government said she didn't make enough money."

Age 31 – My mother's cousin refuses to accept money that a rich
woman left him. He says the money has too much blood on it.
My mother tells me that in 1939 her cousin had asked this woman
to sign affidavits for his wife and two daughters. She said no.

Age 33 – My father asks me to dial the number. His hands shake. He asks my cousin Judy if she wants to send her three children out of Israel during the Gulf War. She says she can't let them go.

Age 42 – A waiter in a Jerusalem hotel tells my father he should come to live in Israel, because it's home. My father tells him, "Home is anywhere they let you in."

Regarding Niederstetten, Shabbos Morning, March 25, 1933

Opa Kirchheimer Speaks

Three storm troopers came into our house
searching for weapons. In the *Guteszimmer*,
the room we used for special occasions,
I saw my wife showing them my army photograph
from World War I and my Iron Cross medal.
One storm trooper asked if I had stolen it.
They arrested me and took two pairs
of my wife's good leather gloves.

My brother-in-law Wolf Braun, my friends Fritz Neuburger,
Max Stern, Michael Levi, Siegfried Schlesinger, Herman Braun,
Leopold Schlossberger, and I were taken to Town Hall, gagged and
blindfolded, taken one at a time into a room, made to lie
face down on chairs, beaten from our heels to our necks
by six gendarmes using steel rods and rubber hoses.
Then they made us stand in front of a burning
coal stove until we passed out.
Two hours later I was released. I dragged myself home
on the side roads so I wouldn't be seen.

His Son Speaks

I heard them from my bedroom, got dressed, and came downstairs.
I saw my mother in the *Guteszimmer* with the storm troopers, saw
them take my father away.

My mother, sister, and little brother waited at home, and I walked
to shul to see who else had been taken.

Sunday morning, I went to see Onkel Wolf.
"Look at me so you won't forget what happened,"
and he showed me his body.
"At least you have some clear skin," I said. "My father doesn't have any."

On Sunday morning our neighbors said the Protestant minister,
Pastor Umfrid, told his congregation what had been done
to the Jews was wrong, told them the Jews survived the Romans
and would survive the Nazis.
Two days later, Nazi leaders told him to retract his speech.
He refused, was beaten, arrested, and put in jail.
Three weeks later, the Nazis said he committed suicide.

Summary Afternoon, 1934

"There was a camp," my father tells me,
"about three kilometers from our town,
where young men lived, part of

Arbeitsdienst, the national labor service, constructing
the Autobahn, bridges, and flood-control dikes.
About a hundred men marched by our house

on the way back to the camp, in their uniforms,
carrying spades, singing, '*Wenn das Juden blut
von dem Messer spritz*,' when Jewish blood sprays from the knife,

'*dann gehts nochmals so gut*,' it will be much better.
Onkel Max and I watched them march by.
'They can't do more than kill us,' Onkel Max said."

Keeping Watch, 1936

"I slept on the chaise lounge in his room," my father told me.
"Grossvater didn't want to stay alone anymore.
He was afraid the Hitler Jugend would throw stones at his windows.

My feet hung over the chaise, so I put a chair at the end.
I was getting tall.
'Some *shomer*, some watcher,' Grossvater would say each morning.

I didn't hear a thing at night.
I was fifteen years old.
I slept like the dead."

Traces

"Sometimes we had to let chickens die of old age,"
my father says. "It was against the law to have meat
kosher-killed, but sometimes the *shochet*, Gerson Rosenthal,
gave me his knife after *shacharis*.

I hid it in a pocket of my lederhosen and rode my bike home.
At night, Gerson came to the front door carrying
a pen and paper, to look like he was collecting for charity,
and my mother and I carried a few chickens to the cellar.

He slaughtered them.
My mother plucked the feathers and gave him some meat
to take home, while I buried the blood in the garden
and the feathers at the bottom of the manure pile next to the barn.

I didn't pour the blood into the brook behind our house.
Someone might see it floating.
The next morning I put the knife back in my lederhosen,
rode my bike to shul, and returned it to Gerson.

My mother canned the meat and served it only on a holiday.
We only had the *shochet* come when my father wasn't home.
He didn't want us to do anything that would get us arrested
and never knew what we'd done until he came to the table."

Berlin to Hamburg, Summer, 1938

They slept in haystacks,
four boys on a bike trip,
stole potatoes, prayed with tallis
and tefillin each morning
in fields. Farmers chased them out.

They rode fast, wearing lederhosen
and caps, Brownshirt boys
chasing them.

My father met an old Gypsy woman
by a roadside. She told him, "You
must be one of us, black hair, black eyes,
dark skin. The Germans must have stolen you."

In Hamburg, he visited his aunt,
Tante Therese. She made him
"tea with milk, just like the English," for the first time.
He didn't know it would be the last.

Town Hall

"What for?" my father asked. "What
did I do? I'm only sixteen," and
the gendarme told him if he didn't

like it, if he asked any more questions, he could go home,
they'd arrest his father instead. And he saw his father
paying his tax bill in the next room,

and he didn't call out, afraid they'd arrest him too, afraid
his father would want to take his place, and
the gendarme said he had a job to do, a quota of ten men,

and he didn't care how he filled it. And my father
knew the gendarme, went to school with his daughter.
He was told to empty his pockets, turn

in any money and weapons, and he turned in
his pocketknife, and told the gendarme he had to go
to the bathroom, and another gendarme, Wilhelm,

took him, and he knew Wilhelm too. He told Wilhelm
not to worry, he wasn't going to run away, and
Wilhelm said he knew, but he was doing his job.

As my father and nine men were loaded on a truck
that said "*Trink* Coca-Cola" he turned and saw
Wilhelm crying like a child.

Breaking Laws

Kristallnacht
broken glass
Nazis arrest him
a boy sixteen years old

Dachau
November 1938
a striped cotton uniform
it's almost winter

he shares a bunk
with a man in his fifties
who freezes to death one night

the next morning a kapo tells him
take off the man's long underwear
do it quickly
before the SS come for the body
you will freeze at night too
if you don't

it is the custom of some Jews
not to wear clothes from a dead body
and to save one's life the rabbis teach
one must break custom

he washes the underwear that night
places it over a chair
next to the woodstove to dry
sleeps on it
still damp
to make sure
no one will steal it

Lines

My father stood in line to be photographed, stood
in line to be fingerprinted, stood in line
to have his head shaved.

"You're young to be here,"
a kapo told him as he got to the front of another line,
and gave his name, hometown, age, occupation, and he saw

men standing in another line, saw men standing,
naked, on a concrete slab, and the kapo told my father, "Hold
your breath when the SS aim the fire hoses at your mouth, if you don't

you'll swallow water, choke, lose
your balance, the SS will gang up on you,
they're only kids, they'll get a kick out of it."

He stood in line to strip. Naked, he stood in line
to turn in his winter coat, his clothes, his shoes.
He stood in line to stand on the concrete slab.

If You Were Lucky

you got a hat, my father said. Told to strip,
he stood in line, got examined by an SS doctor
for skin diseases and bruises, told to go,
then got beaten by an SS guard, stood

in line to get a blue-and-white-striped
cotton jacket and pants, yellow triangles
stenciled on each,
leather shoes with no linings,

a pair of cotton socks,
two patches with numbers,
a cotton blue-and-white-striped hat,
was marched to his barracks, given

a needle and thread, was told to sew
one patch on his shirt,
the other on his pants,
and pass the needle to the next man,

and each morning was marched out to line up
between the barracks at four o'clock, was counted, stood
until the kapos marched him
to the *Appellplatz*, for roll call, stood

at attention for hours, was told by the *Kommandant*
to put his hand on his head, take off his hat and,
at the *Kommandant's* command, slap it down on his thigh.
Thousands of us, my father said. Sounded like a cannon shot.

Testing Ground

And my father told me he was sent
into a room with high ceilings.
He was told to sit with his legs wide open,
the next man told to sit inside his legs.
And the next, and the next.
He sat until the SS finished counting
how many would fit in the room.
It was 8,000.

A Good Job

I

"I'd shine their shoes at night and put them under their beds
so they'd pick me," my father says.

"I was in *Baracke* 18, *Stube* 1, almost 2,000 men in each *Stube*, racks
of bunks. When the bunks were full, straw mattresses on the floor. If
the kapos picked me to sweep, wash and polish the floors, I wouldn't
have to stand out in the cold.

Each morning, at four o'clock, we were marched outside.
We sang songs for hours in the cold. The songs were taped, played
on the radio to show how happy, how well taken care of, we were.

An SS officer would come into the barracks, check my work,
and I stood at attention, took off my hat, did not speak
unless spoken to. Sometimes he
told me to continue and left."

II

"I'd volunteer to be a *Kostträger*, a food carrier.
While the others waited in the roll-call line, three of us carried
two cast-iron buckets, enough to hold vegetable soup for 1,000 men.
Two would hold the handles on the outside. I was in the middle,

holding the handles on the insides. A kapo marched us
one half mile from the kitchen to the space between the barracks
where army bread, *Kommissbrot*, was piled up
like bricks on the tables where we ate.
The kapos said, 'Kirchheimer is the best *Kostträger* we have.'

Some men wouldn't eat the soup, saying it wasn't kosher, but I ate it.
I knew they wouldn't put any meat in it."

A Simple Gesture

"It was December. Four o'clock in the morning.
The air clear and cold.
I could see the Bavarian Alps.
I stood in the roll-call line next to Dr. Spatz.
The SS would pick on him.

A lieutenant asked him, 'If I were to shoot you now,
what would you do about it?'
He gave the SS officer's rank, gave his own, the same
as all Jewish prisoners', *Schutzhaftjude*, protected Jew,
then spoke: 'I could not do anything.'"

Once, Dr. Spatz answered without giving the SS officer's rank.
He knocked off the doctor's glasses, beat him in the face.
My father waited until the SS officer left,
picked up the glasses, and gave them back to Dr. Spatz.

String

"I sneaked out one night," my father tells me,
"waited for the searchlights to pass and ran
to see Onkel Max three barracks away.
I gave him some newspaper and string.
He was mad at me, afraid I would get in trouble.

One morning I got caught. During roll call, an SS officer
saw newspaper sticking out from my shoes.
He found it tied around my legs with string.

He made me take off all the newspaper and pile it up
in front of him. He yelled at me for using it to keep warm.
He told the kapos to make anyone else wearing newspaper
put it in the pile.
Then I was let go.
I was lucky that day."

Shopping in Dachau

The SS ran a store in Dachau.
It sold long underwear, gloves, and baked goods
and was open only at night.

Prisoners were allowed ten marks
to be sent to them each month, and
prisoners were not allowed
out of the barracks at night.

Once, my father's parents sent him money.
He sneaked out at night, bought
a chocolate éclair, ate it so fast he vomited.
He never went back to the store.

One Night

A man went crazy in the barracks.
"We told him to stop," my father said.
"We told him the SS would take him.
We tried to stop his screaming, his flailing arms.

The kapos heard him, came and tried to restrain him.
They took him into the latrine, put his head under water.
They couldn't stop his screaming, his flailing arms.

They called from kapo to kapo, from barracks to barracks,
until it reached SS headquarters. The SS came, took him outside.
We heard the hoses turned on him, then a shot. Then we went to sleep."

Hand-me-down Clothing

"We always had hope we would get out," my father tells me.
"Some mornings at the roll call between the barracks, a kapo
would call names of prisoners being
released that day, telling them to step forward.
One morning a kapo called 'Kirchheimer,' and I ran to him.
He asked if my first name was Max.
I went back to the line, stood at attention.

One morning, my name was called.
I sneaked to my barracks, took off my long underwear, ran
back to the roll-call line to find Berthold Schlossberger, my father's cousin.
He sneaked to the latrine, put on the long underwear.

Kapos marched us to the *Appellplatz* for the roll call of the entire camp.
The prisoners being released were separated from the others.
I was marched to another building, stood in line to return
the uniform, prisoner numbers, shoes, and get my clothes."

Release from Dachau

"I had a dream last night," my father tells me.
He dreamed the kapos woke him up at four o'clock
in the morning, on Friday, December 23, 1938,
made him strip out of his uniform, made him
wait in line for an SS doctor to examine him

for bruises and frostbite, made him listen to speeches
by the SS warning him to get out of Germany and never
return. They warned him if he didn't, he'd be sent back to Dachau
and never leave. He dreamed he was assigned a place
in another line, waited to return his uniform and get his own clothes,
shoes and coat, and that the SS drove him to an area about four miles
from the Munich train station, then made him march the rest of the way.

The sky was so black, he couldn't see the man who gave him a ticket.
It took twelve hours, and he changed trains twice.
He had no money, no food.
The train arrived on Shabbos morning, and he didn't want to see
another person's face and took the back way home through the fields,
crossing eight railroad tracks, careful not to get caught

in the track switches. His father was the first person to see him
as he opened the shutters he closed each night so no one could throw
rocks into the house. He went through the front gate into the house,
saw his mother had baked challahs, and ate an entire one. He went to sleep
at eleven o'clock in the morning and slept until the next day.

"That's exactly how it happened," my father tells me.
"That's how I got home.
Can you believe I still dream about it sixty years later?"

Getting a Visa

"The doctor made me strip," my father said,
"listened to my heart and lungs, made me
walk down the hall to see
if I limped,

sent me to another room, where I waited
while others were called, watched
as each raised his right hand, as each received
a piece of paper.

My name was called, I stood up,
raised my hand, answered '*Ja.*'
The man laughed at me.
I didn't understand what he said,
but he gave me the piece of paper.

Visa, U.S. Consulate, Stuttgart, a red ribbon
attached to the corner.

I heard teenagers in America wore white shoes in summer.
I went to a shoe store.
I wanted to be in style."

My Father's Sister

In an old black-and-white photograph
Ruth looked just like Dorothy
with long, dark braids
and a small black dog on her lap.

But it was not Kansas, and
she could not click her heels
three times and go home.
She did not own
a pair of ruby slippers,

and the yellow brick road
did not lead to the gates
of the Emerald City.
It led to the gates
of Auschwitz.

Josef

"Josef and my mother waved goodbye
as I got on the train. My mother held Josef's hand.
It was the last time I saw them.

He was ten years younger, but he was my buddy.
I would take him on the back of my bike to school each day, riding
as fast as I could, so the Brownshirts wouldn't catch him,"

and I want to pick Josef up, rock and sing him to sleep,
Guten Abend, Gute Nacht, lay him down gently in his bed,
push the hair out of his eyes, kiss him goodnight, and say
the bedtime prayer with him, *Hamal'ach hago'el oti mikol ra
y'varech et hane'arim v'yikaray bahem sh'mi v'shaym avotai
Avraham v'Yitzchak v'yidgu larov b'kerev ha'aretz,*
the angel who redeems me from all evil,
bless the young boys, and may they multiply.

II

Setting Out

It is not permitted to set out on a ship less than three days
before Shabbos. This is said only for a voluntary purpose.
For a mitzvah, it is permitted.
          —*Babylonian Talmud: Shabbos 19a.*

"I almost lost all my photographs," my father tells me.
"My mother, sister, and brother brought me on Thursday
to the train in Niederstetten.
I got off in Aachen and waited with others for the Antwerp train.
The Gestapo pulled me out, searched my luggage, my family photographs,
told me to take off my shoes and socks, searched them, let me go.
I missed the train and waited two hours for the next one.

Shabbos morning, I walked to the boat.
My name was called on the loudspeaker, and I reported to the purser
who said my large suitcase wasn't sent from the train station.
He would drive me there if I wanted.
If I didn't return on time, I would miss the ship,
but those photographs were all I had. I found my suitcase,
and the purser drove as fast as he could back to the ship.
I climbed the gangplank, about four stories high, with my suitcase,
and as I got close to the deck, a dockworker pushed the gangplank away.
With all my might, I threw the suitcase on deck and jumped on the ship.

A Chinese fellow and I played shuffleboard and Ping-Pong.
We couldn't talk to each other, but we understood each other.
It was before I made new friends, before I met your mother.
The Nazi government allowed emigres to leave with ten U.S. dollars.
I spent three in Antwerp, one aboard ship.
Aunt Elsie came to the docks in Hoboken and took me to the Bronx.
I came to America on August 29, 1939, with six dollars and my life."

37

House of Cards

"There was Cockeyed Newman, the Widow Feingold, and Shayna Dora. They played cards every day in Aunt Elsie's kitchen, at 1266 Grand Concourse, arriving at exactly four in the afternoon. Uncle Harry and I would have to wait for supper until they finished playing. Uncle Harry and I finally got sick of having the card players in the kitchen, so we got a plan. We decided to get the Widow Feingold married off. We put an ad in *Der Tag*, 'Rich widow looking for husband.' Louie the Gold Digger answered the ad and a short time later they were married and moved to Florida, so he could spend all her money. That ended the game.

"Bob the Undertaker and his wife, Fanny *die Bumbel*, lived upstairs. We called her that because she was round like a bumblebee. She was a yenta and had to know everything that went on in the building. Aunt Elsie knew everything, so *die Bumbel* spent more time in Elsie's kitchen than in her own. *Die Bumbel* asked Aunt Elsie if she minded that I was living with them. Aunt Elsie said she wasn't too happy I was there. 'Who needs it,' she said. I didn't let on that I understood. Uncle Harry and Aunt Elsie helped me learn English, helped me fill out affidavits for my mother, father, brother, and sister, and agreed to be sponsors. They listed the income from the boarders they took in on the affidavits, but they didn't list the money Uncle Harry made from painting apartments. They thought the government would make them pay taxes. The government said they didn't make enough money to support four more people.

"One day *die Bumbel* and Aunt Elsie were talking about me and *die Bumbel* said, 'I can see it in his eyes, he understands, he understands!' Aunt Elsie told me she didn't see what all the fuss was about the visas. 'It couldn't be that bad. Everyone was afraid the Jews wouldn't return after World War I, and they all came back.'"

Greenhorn

"It was my first job, the American Automatic Venetian Blind Corporation
of Brooklyn, $16 a week, a feeder or catcher, making
blinds out of wood, taking slats off a pile, feeding them two at a time
into a painting machine or catching them as they came out
and standing them up to dry. During lunch,
the Italian guys taught me to play baseball in an empty lot.
I got a hit, was rounding third, heading home,
and they yelled, 'Run, Guggie, run like hell,' and I did.
They clapped me on the back, 'You made it,
you made it,' but I didn't know what I had made.
They thought my last name was Guggenheimer.
They thought it sounded like Kirchheimer.
They thought I was rich and asked why
I needed work with a name like that. After,
we'd storm into Phil's: 10¢ for a sandwich and 5¢ for a bottle of Pepsi.
There was only room for ten, but thirty of us piled in.
Phil, an old guy from Poland, yelled, 'Boyes, be qviet,'
and the Italians yelled back, 'Aw, shuddup
or we won't come in here anymore.'
The Italian guys danced on top of the tables, while the Jewish guys
wondered who'd get laid off next. I brought my own lunch,
but treated myself to a Pepsi. I needed to save money,
needed to show the government how much I had in the bank,
so they would let me bring my family over.
The Italian guys taught me when to run, when to stay,
and how to keep score. They were so tough,
so free. They didn't take shit from anybody.
One guy invited me to go fishing Sunday afternoons.
'You come to my house in Canarsie, Guggie.
I'll introduce you to some girls.'
I never went. I didn't know how to get there
from the Bronx and was too ashamed to ask."

Western Union

WHAT HATH GOD WROUGHT
—the first telegraphic message wired in Morse code, 1844.

1936
HAVE ARRIVED SAFELY IN HAIFA
My father's brother to his mother, father, two sisters,
and three brothers in Germany

1939
HAVE ARRIVED SAFELY IN NEW YORK
My father to his family remaining in Germany

1940
ATTEMPTED BOOKING SIMON RUTH KIRCHHEIMER
AMERICA LINE FROM LISBON NOT POSSIBLE
NEW BOOKING DEPARTURE DATE NOT CERTAIN
REPLY BY TELEGRAM
My father's father and sister from Stuttgart to my father in New York

1940
CAN YOU REACH LISBON
READY TO FORWARD MONEY FOR TICKETS
THROUGH AMERICAN EXPRESS
REPLY BY TELEGRAM
My father in New York by return

No reply
Stop

The Photograph in My Hand

My mother, four years old, blond curls,
wearing a smocked dress, in a field of goldenrod,
her doll on her lap and her dog at her side.

Two years later, the girl in the photograph
would be backed up against a wall at school,
by kids in her class for refusing to say "Heil Hitler,"

and they would throw rocks, beat her up, call her *Jude*,
her dress would be torn, and her parents
would have to find a way to get her out of Germany.

She would be sent to an orphanage in Amsterdam,
and they would wait two years for their visas
to America. I want to ask the girl what

would have become of her if her parents hadn't
found a way out? Would she have survived?
Would she have been experimented on like her cousin Hanni

who returned home after the war and rarely
left her room, or would she,
like another cousin, Bertl, have tried to cross the Pyrenees

into Spain and never be heard from again? What if Hitler had never come
to power, would she and her parents still have come to America?
Would she have met my father, and who would

she have married if she had stayed in Germany, and
who would she have become and what would have become
of me? I cannot let go of it.

Retelling

You shall explain to your child on that day, it is because of
what God did for me that I went free from Egypt.
—*Exodus 13:8.*

In Frankfurt, my Oma Strauss bought new Haggadoth
for their first Pesach seder in America.

The storekeeper didn't think she was Jewish and
asked why she wanted the books.

She told him, "*B'chol dor va'dor*, in every generation,
one must regard himself as if he had personally gone out from Egypt.

When I am on the ship, I will tell my daughter Margot
the story of why the Jews must leave this country."

The Way to a Visa

My mother tells me of the train
ride to the American Consulate in Stuttgart
when she was eight years old,
and of the jewelry that her mother owned,

and of the window her mother opened at every bridge,
of the rings, bracelets, and necklaces she threw out
when Jews were ordered to turn in their gold
and silver, saving only her wedding ring.

My mother tells me of the doctor who makes her undress
and makes her mother leave the room.
He listens to her heart, checks for marks and bruises, and
she tells me of the shiny metal object he uses as he spreads her legs.

The visa was stamped, a red ribbon attached to its corner.
And my mother tells me of the red Mary Jane shoes her mother
buys her on the way back to the train and of her excitement
at seeing the statue of the Lorelei for the first time.

She tells me of the legend every German schoolchild learns,
and I sit in the kitchen, listening as my seventy-year-old mother sings me
her song: "I do not know what it should mean that I am so sad,
a legend from old days past that will not go out from my mind."

My Mother's Sister, Resi

She will tell you, if you ask, she was born
in the resort town of Bad Salzschlirf in the state of Hessen,
and that her childhood was ordinary, except once

a photographer asked if she would be his model.
She still has the pictures. She likes the one
with her arms draped around her mother's neck,
and they are smiling. She will tell you about her mother, who would say
some things do not stay just on your clothes, they go deeper.

If you ask what her life was like in the thirties,
she will tell you she had to leave Germany, that the Gestapo
came to the home where she was working as a *Kindermädchen*
and wanted to see the owner, Mr. Levi.
She said he was away on business and did not know
when he would return, then phoned him in Switzerland

and told him not to come back. She left
for Amsterdam and worked as a maid for the Roos family,
who gave her their concert tickets when they could not attend.
She heard Yehudi Menuhin give one of his first performances.
She doesn't remember what he played, but she can still

hear the sounds from his violin.
She came to America alone in November of 1939
sailing through mined waters in the Atlantic, settling
in Connecticut with her parents and little sister.

A man from Russia, a cattle dealer, asked to marry her.
They had five children.
One son died forty-three years ago from leukemia.
You will see the black-and-white photographs
of their older children, taken at the beach, and of the younger ones,

on their farm, that hang over her bed in the nursing home.
She wants to go to sleep and not wake up.
She says she is as useless as an old box,
no longer able to see, and her fingers are crippled by arthritis.
You will see a woman who gave up after her eldest son

committed suicide six years ago. As you leave, if you turn around,
you will see her sitting in a chair in the solarium, watching
nothing in particular. But you will not see what she is thinking.

This Is How My Opa Strauss Died

He walked home from work in the blizzard of '47.
My Oma opened the door.
"Natan, why are you carrying groceries in this weather?"
"I always bring you something, Jenny," he said,
and collapsed in her arms.

But the dying began long before, when
he was forced to sell his butcher shop
after Hitler came to power, when
he saw his six-year-old daughter
beaten up by schoolchildren for refusing
to say "Heil Hitler," when
he was forced to sell his beloved horses,

his home, his land, when
he was seasick on the S.S. Roosevelt
for the ten days it took to cross the Atlantic
from Le Havre to New York City, when
he stood on cold concrete warehouse floors
as a night watchman in Harlem, when

the Hebrew Immigrant Aid Society got him
a job as a farmer's helper in Connecticut and
he wouldn't tell the owner he had a heart condition, when
he sat alone in a corner of the greenhorn section
of shul each Shabbos, when

he found out after the war he would never see
any of his nine brothers and sisters again, when
he worked as a meat cutter through each heart attack, when
he walked up Meadow Street and his neighbor Rose DeNegris,
eight months pregnant, saw him carrying a bag of groceries, asked
why he was out in such weather, he said,
"I don't have long to live."

The American Branch of the Family

On my mother's dresser is a passport photograph
of her cousin Bertl Katz at thirteen.

My mother's family tried to get her out of Germany,
filled out affidavits, tried to sponsor her, but they didn't

make enough money. Cousin Marion had enough money,
but didn't want a greenhorn in her home with her two young sons.

"Bertl escaped to France," my mother told me,
"and tried to cross the Pyrenees into Spain."

Comforts

My father shows me a book Mr. Stern wrote
about Jewish life in Niederstetten.
In one story, Mr. Stern and the nine others
celebrated Shabbos in the district jail with the wine
and challah that his wife asked their jailer to give them.

Mrs. Stern was sure the jailer did.
It was probably something she needed to believe,
so that's the way he wrote it.
My father asks if I want to know the truth.

The jailer asked what they wanted to eat.
They said they wouldn't eat non-kosher food
and asked for Bismarck herring.

The Talmud asks: "How does one praise
a bride while dancing in front of her?"

He brought it in a big metal can.
No *kiddush*, no *motzi*.

The school of Shammai says: "Describe her as she is."
The school of Hillel says: "Describe the bride
as beautiful and full of grace."

The jailer spoke to the gendarme
about the food, and was told not to worry,
they wouldn't be here much longer. "Monday
they go to Dachau."

"But suppose she is lame or blind. Is one to say,
Oh bride, beautiful and full of grace, seeing
that Scripture says, Keep far from a false word?
The Sages say: The disposition of man should always
be pleasant towards others."

And sometimes I see Mr. Stern telling his wife
after his release that the challah she baked
was light and fluffy and made him feel
like he was at home for Shabbos,

and sometimes I wish my father
would speak to me like Mr. Stern.

Brothers

Bule is what my father's little brother, Josef,
used to call him when they were kids.

Sometimes I have trouble remembering
that my father got to be a kid,
that there was a time

when he hadn't gotten a note in his report card
saying that Jews could no longer attend school
with Aryan children, when he didn't get chased
off the field for playing soccer with the other kids,

when he didn't see the "Jews not welcome"
sign at the public pool, and he and his friends
didn't have brown-shirted boys chasing
after them on a bike trip,

and sometimes I wonder what it
would be like if Josef were able to call.

Birthday Wishes

When I turned seventeen and blew out the candles
on my birthday cake, I wished for clothes,
a car, a boyfriend.

When my father turned seventeen, he got
a ration of butter for his bread.
Dr. Spatz had told a kapo, "It's the kid's birthday."

Opa Kirchheimer

As a child I wished you
had survived Auschwitz, survived
each selection, survived
the work details, the experiments.

I wished you were liberated at the end
of the war, were stuck behind the Iron Curtain,
had amnesia and couldn't remember us,
or didn't know how to find us in America.

I wished one day you'd knock on our front door
and tell me what my father was like as a boy.

Tell Me, Josef

Do you know that the clouds of summer still
give way to the clear skies of fall, that at

sunset the horizon seems to tumble from blue,
pink, and orange to black ink that spills

across the sky, and do you know that I dream
you were liberated from Auschwitz, that you

returned to Maastricht and visited your friend Paul, and
he returned the leather schoolbag you gave him

the night before you were deported, and
he gave you the four postcards you sent him

from Westerbork before you were sent to Auschwitz, and
do you know that the postcards you wrote

were given by Paul to the Joods Historisch Museum in Amsterdam, and
I found copies on the Internet, and do you know

I will travel to the museum this January to meet Paul and
see the words you wrote as an eleven-year-old,

the words that are here now in place of you, and
tell me, Josef, do you know that sometimes

in the middle of the night, I look out the window
and watch the sky and

I see rain begin to fall and watch
more fall down?

Found: Four Postcards to a Friend Before Deportation to Auschwitz

Westerbork Camp, Holland, *Barak* 43K

5 September 1942
To Paul Lardinois, Maastricht, Holland

We arrived here well.
I go to school here.
Do you get any fruit? We get none.
Perhaps you can write me some news from Maastricht.
Also a lot of greetings to your parents, Harrie, and Robbie,
and a lot of greetings to Jan, David, Leo, Guus.
Write soon.
From your friend, Josef Kirchheimer
Also kind regards from my parents and my sister.

19 September 1942

Dear Paul,
Many thanks for your letter
and for that nice and good package.
I was very happy with it.
Also many thanks to your parents.
I would have written instantly, but we may write
only once every fourteen days.
We again have rainy weather.
I eagerly go to school here.
A lot of greetings to you and your parents.
From your friend, Josef.
Also a lot of greetings from my parents.

9 October 1942

Dear Paul,
I hope you received my postcard.
How are you and your parents?
I hope you are well.
We also are healthy.
Paul, can you perhaps send me some batteries,
two of those round ones and two of those square ones.
I would be very thankful to you.
Often we play soccer with a leather ball.
For today I don't have more to say.
Kindest regards from your friend, Josef.

18 October 1942

Dear Paul,
I received your package and postcard.
Thank you very much.
I was so happy with it.
Everything was delicious, especially the cake.
Can you send me a tube of glue?
Also we have had bad colds,
all of us, and were bedridden.
We are doing better again now.
Kind regards from your friend Josef.
Also warm greetings from my parents and sister and many thanks.

Thursday Afternoon at the Joods Historisch Museum, Amsterdam

I sit on a bench on the second floor of the museum
built on the ruins of four synagogues,
their interiors destroyed by the Nazis,

watching a movie, projected on a white wall,
a montage of Jewish life
in Holland during the war.

A wedding. Yellow stars sewn on overcoats.
People leaving the hall.
People jammed into cattle cars.

Deportations to Westerbork. Two men shaking
hands as if they will meet again soon.
The doors slam. Steel bars lock.

I watch the footage over and over.
Hoping to find Oma, Opa.
Maybe even Ruth or Josef.

Maybe one face.
One last glance.
One last handshake.

But tears blur the faces
of the people getting on the trains.
And I can no longer see if you are there.

Passages

"Josef gave me his leather schoolbag," Paul tells me.
"He and his parents and Ruth came to say goodbye

the night before they were deported to Westerbork."
I tell my father, and he asks if Paul still has the bag.

I tell him that Paul used it for school and then for work,
but it doesn't exist anymore.

"That was my schoolbag," my father tells me.
"I gave it to Josef the night before I left for America."

In Oma Kirchheimer's Hand

In Gothic script
on paper now so brittle—
almost sixty years old—
it falls apart at the touch.

Meine lieben Kinder!, my beloved
children, she writes
to the ones
who made it to America,

and I cannot read any further.
I know how it will end.

Cost of Life, America, 1944

In the summer of that year, a Jewish child's life was not worth
the two-fifths of a cent it would have cost to put it to death
by gassing rather than burn it alive.
—*Rabbi Irving "Yitz" Greenberg,*
Cloud of Smoke, Pillar of Fire.

Loaf of bread   8¢
Gallon of milk   62¢
Roll of toilet paper   5¢
One dozen eggs   54¢
Gallon of gasoline   18¢

Holocaust Victim Assets Litigation Initial Questionnaire

A) Claimant: Julius Kirchheimer

B) Address prior to Nazi occupation: Hindenburg Strasse 341, Niederstetten, Germany

C) Filing For: Father, mother, sister, brother

D) Date and place of death(s): 5 November 1942, Auschwitz

E) Type of Class Member: Jewish

F) Looted Assets Claim Against Swiss Persons or Entities:

Assets: means any and all objects of value including but not limited to personal, commercial, real, tangible and intangible property.

Looted Assets	Value
Man's gold pocket watch	$100
Young woman's needlework	$ 37
Gold wedding rings	$165
Boy's bicycle	$ 64
Gold fillings in teeth	$ 48
Silver Shabbos candlesticks	$ 87

This questionnaire is for information purposes only.
Completion does not automatically entitle you to receive payments.
Please note, compensation for loss of life is specifically excluded.

It Has Been Reported

Swiss banks laundered money and gold for the Nazis.
I ask my mother if any of our relatives had money in Swiss banks.
She says no.
I ask my father.
He tells me his mother had gold in her teeth.

Justice

130,681 survivors will receive 401 million dollars from
a restitution fund for slave laborers. Six decades [after the war],
most are no longer around to collect.
  —*Clyde Haberman, New York Times, August 3, 2004.*

This is about money.
But not exactly.
This is about righting an old wrong.
But not entirely.
This is about making peace
with history.
But not really.

In the name of the German people, Johannes Rau,
Germany's president, begs forgiveness.

Sure, this is about money.
But not exactly.
We're restituting money. We're restituting history,
claims Gideon Taylor of the Claims Conference.
The research into verifying the claims is now
a tool for historians.

Yes, it is about righting a wrong.
But not entirely.
Aron Krell says this money can
never compensate him
for his lost family and childhood.

Is it really about making peace with history?
Not really.
There are limits to everything.

Even forgiveness.

III

Missing

The sound of Ruth's voice
My paternal grandmother and grandfather
All my mother's cousins
Her uncle Sali
My father's high-school education
His birth certificate
Family reunions

If

---

schoolkids hadn't backed my mother, six years old at the time,
   against a wall, thrown rocks at her, and called her *Jude*.
my aunt hadn't escaped to Holland and worked as a maid
   to make enough money to get my mother out of Germany.
my mother hadn't had to live in an orphanage in Amsterdam and
   wait until my grandparents could get immigration visas.
my mother hadn't had to return to Germany to get her visa for America.
my father hadn't had to leave his home and family to immigrate
   to America.
the United States government hadn't had immigration quotas.
the United States hadn't made him, a seventeen-year-old, fill out
   affidavit after affidavit after affidavit.
the Nazis hadn't invaded Holland one day before
   his father and sister were to leave for America.
the boat they were supposed to be on hadn't been bombed in the harbor.
they hadn't been sent to the left instead of the right.
life didn't depend on if.

How to Spot One of Us

We're the ones who didn't know our relatives
spoke with accents, the ones whose parents
got nervous if we didn't come home
on time, were afraid to let us go
places by ourselves, who
told the neighborhood kids the numbers

on their forearms were their phone numbers,
who won't visit Germany, who wake up
night after night from dreams, who never talk
about the past, or never stop
talking about the past, and we're the ones

who dream about big families, who
wish words could just be words, wish "camp"
or "selection" didn't make us flinch,
and sometimes we're the ones
who do everything we can
so you don't know who we are.

Lunchtime

Sometimes I can't eat pizza.
It's the ovens.
I want to scream, but the sounds
never come up from my throat.

Bon appétit, says my companion
biting into a slice.

At the Butcher's

Take a number please,
the dispenser reads
at the butcher's.
I take one and wait in line.
It's before Shabbos, everyone is rushed,
people pushing or being pushed,
trying to get to the counter, to get their food,
someone mutters, "I was ahead of you."

"Who's next?" says the butcher,
and panic falls from me like a puzzle
dropped on the floor and I can't
find all the pieces and the ones I can
pick up don't fit together anymore and

I want to tell them about my father's
sister and how her visa number was too
high and there were too many people in
line ahead of her waiting to get out and how
she was deported to
Auschwitz and she didn't get
a number there and if she had, she
might have survived and

I want to tell them about my friend's mother, how
she got a number on her forearm in
Auschwitz, and how she got a
visa number after the war and about the
dreams she has every night and

the butcher calls my number, and I
cannot make a sound.

Jury Duty

"Welcome to jury duty.
We'll try to make this as painless
as possible," says the officer in charge.
He means it as a joke.
I notice he carries a gun.

I begin to knit, knit one,
purl two, knit one, purl two,
the needles click-clack.

He announces we are about to begin
the selection process.
I drop a stitch.
"If I call your name report to the left."
He calls my name.

On My Way to Work

I see a woman walking
her German shepherd.
The dog turns its head
to follow my movements.
As they pass,
I hold my breath.

Waiting

I wait at Kennedy International Arrivals
for my cousin Rachel.
Her flight from Israel is on time, listed on the arrivals board,
and I'm certain she will come out soon.
I search the faces that have come through customs.

The flight is taken off the arrivals board, and I wait.

> My father's brother Arthur goes to the docks,
> almost every day, from 1942 to 1945, watches
> the ships come in, checks the manifests
> to see if anyone made it to Haifa. My father,
> his brother Bruno, his sister Rita wait
> in New York for a letter, a telegram.

Rachel calls my name, and I turn,
hug her, crying, not wanting to let go,
not able to tell her why.

Grand Central Station

A packed subway car
at rush hour
more people try
to jam themselves
in before the doors
slam shut.

Move in move in make room
just one
more they shout.

How Mengele
would smile
if he could see this.

Rooms on the Left, Rooms on the Right

I see spotlights and fences and people standing in lines
to go into rooms on the left and rooms on the right,
and I hear a woman tell her children, "Stay with me,
we don't want to get separated," and my heart
begins to pound, and I walk out of the lobby
of the U.S. Holocaust Memorial Museum
and look up at the sky in Washington and try to find the sun.

Inside a Cattle Car

Perhaps the dead wondered
why I traveled so far when
I stayed only a short time.

I stood outside a cattle car
brought from Poland, and tried to
slow my breath, to find a way to enter.

Hundreds of voices assaulted me.
They wanted to tell me their stories. In this car,
31 feet long, 14 feet high, 13 feet wide.

I could not understand any of them,
the noise too loud, too rough.
I was frightened. I did not want

to know, to hear any more. Perhaps
the dead were angry. I entered
but would not listen to what they said.

The Promised Land

When my father went to Israel, he found
Bertl Rosenthal, the *shochet's* daughter, in a nursing home.
It had been thirty years.
She almost didn't recognize him,
couldn't believe he'd come to visit.

He asked how she felt, if she slept at night.
She took his arm, and told him, "Most of the time.
When I can't," she said, "I go through the houses
in our town one by one and remember."

Daughter of Holocaust Survivors

Taking up space
   wherever I am

         taking up space walking to work

taking up space while others may not notice

               writing about not getting on crowded
   subway cars

            seeing connections everywhere
      trying to understand the value of words
            and feeling I knew things before I was born

taking up space because God wants me to, because God wants
   his children to defeat him

               taking up more space each time I write
      taking up less
            contracting
      each time I do not

taking up space because that is one of God's names

Learning to Swim

A father must teach his child to swim in water.
What is the reason? Her life may depend on it.
            —*Babylonian Talmud: Kiddushin 30b.*

I was a small girl and quiet,
so I didn't say anything
when Sandy's mother told me not to tell anyone
I was Jewish, as I climbed into the back
seat of their wood-paneled station wagon,
my bathing suit on under my clothes.

I can't tell you anything about the club
and I don't remember if I went swimming,
but I know I felt something was wrong
with me and that Sandy's mother thought
she was being nice, taking me to a country club.

When I got out of the car, they asked me
if I'd had a nice time. I don't think I said anything
but I do remember their smiles and that I
never went to their club again.

Family History

The doctor comes in, introduces himself,
asks questions about my health (good),
recent illnesses (none), operations
(tonsils removed when I was four), maternal
grandparents (grandmother died at ninety-two from old age,
grandfather died at sixty-six from a heart attack),
paternal grandparents (died before I was born).

The doctor says it is important for my medical history
to know how they died.
So I tell him they died in Auschwitz.
He has no more questions and tells me
to undress for the physical exam.

Imprints

From the womb a fetus looks and can see from the beginning
of the world to its end, and when she emerges, God hits her
under the nose and she forgets everything she saw.
          —Adapted from *Seder Y'tzirat Hav'lad.*

I remember my father driving to the hospital, my mother
yelling at him to slow down, afraid the police

would stop them, the nurses telling him to go home,
it would be a long time, and the nurses wheeling her

into the delivery room, her screams, the drugs,
my father back after only two hours,

and I remember the red roses he brought her,
her asking how much they cost, they had no money, and

my mother's face, her green eyes, her blond hair as she held me,
her olive-skinned girl with a mess of black hair, wondering

if they gave her the wrong baby, and hearing my name,
"Janet," after Oma Kirchheimer, and "Ruth," after my father's sister,

and the woman in the next bed telling my mother
the nurses asked if a Jew could share her room.

Ruth Is My Middle Name

It's Ruth's birthday today.
She was my father's sister.
She died in Auschwitz.

She was twenty-four years old,
three years older than my father.
She taught him about sex, showed him the book

his parents kept on the top shelf of the closet in their bedroom.
I call my father, tell him I remember it's Ruth's birthday, ask him
to tell me something about her that he remembers.

"On the day I left for America, she taught me how to tie my tie.
She came to the station with my mother and brother to say goodbye.
It was the last time I saw them."

He tells me he needs to hang up now.
He needs to start working on his income tax.
"Have fun today," he says.

Rituals

When no one is home, I open the box
and take out one of the five
white linen sheets my father
brings down from the attic
to hang on the walls of our sukkah.

It is still white, and the fabric still strong.
At the bottom are geometric patterns and the initials "RK"
embroidered in white by my father's sister Ruth at fifteen.
The patterns look as if they had been stitched yesterday.

My father brought the sheets with him
to America, while Ruth stayed behind, waiting
for her visa. On the edges

she made buttonholes, the sheets to become the cover
for her comforter made from the finest goose down
that she would take to her marriage, and

as she sits in her bridal chair like a queen
I am dancing in front of her,
fulfilling the mitzvah to make the bride happy,
and she is,

and we dance together,
smiling and laughing, dancing round and round,
until we are out of breath, until I am alone, whirling
in circles, so dizzy I can no longer stand.

What Fathers Tell Sons

My father tells me that in 1933
Nazis beat his father so badly in the neck
he couldn't talk for a week.
His father said not to worry, it would pass.
"I wanted my family to leave Germany,
but I was just a kid, I couldn't say anything."

My father tells me that on Kristallnacht
Nazis broke windows, set homes and businesses on fire.
He and his family hid in the cellar, waiting for the rioting to stop.
"I knew some of them. I went to school with their kids."

When my brother's friends, Shawn, Dikey, and Scott,
stood in our driveway, yelling "Jew, Jew,"
my brother watched from the living room window,
wanting to go outside and beat the crap out of them.
My father said to ignore them, they were just kids.

Some of the Things I Wonder

about the people who live in my father's house.
Do they know Oma Kirchheimer gave birth
to six children in her bedroom?

Can they see the watercress she planted each spring
in the shape of Opa's initials "SK" and can they hear her
speaking to her children, telling them she was giving their father

a *Haarschnitt* each time she cut the watercress, and do they hear them
laughing? Do they know she used the watercress as a border
around the potato salad she made in the kitchen? Is the window box

she filled each spring with pansies, petunias, and nasturtiums
still in the front of the house? Did they find the toys and clothes
left behind, the sukkah stored in the attic?

And if I wanted to see the house, would the new owners let me in
or would I have to stick my foot in the door as Ari Levi did
when he went back to his house and the new people tried to close it on him?

Sisters

My mother's cousin Ilse went to school
with Margot Frank, Anne's older sister.

Sometimes I dream that they met at Ilse's home
on the Schubertstraat and Margot brought her little sister along.

Ilse's mother served them tea and cookies,
and Hanni, Ilse's little sister, played with Anne

and the older girls talked about the boys they liked,
the teachers they didn't, what they would do

during summer vacation, what they would be when they
grew up. Ilse wanted to be a doctor.

Sometimes I dream they were all together
in the same barracks in Bergen Belsen, that Ilse begged

Margot and Anne to live after they contracted typhus, and
that Ilse told them they would get better and

they would meet for tea at a nice café in Amsterdam after the war.
Ilse returned, along with her mother and sister.

They lived in a small apartment, and Hanni, the one who
had been experimented on, rarely came out of her room.

Their father did not survive.
Ilse went back to school and became a doctor.

A Daughter Dreams

I was standing in a line,
sent to the left, but I was still
alive. I should have been
sent to the right, and

I tried to change the dream,
tried to stand in another line
but was sent to the left again and
given a number written
on a piece of paper,
23344,
and it was wrong.

And I went back again, and
I was standing in a line,
sent to the right, and
I got a number, this time
on my arm, and I finally felt better.

Sweet Dreams

Sometimes I dream I'm the one who kills Hitler.
It's simple. I walk up to him,
shoot him in the face, and watch his head
explode into a million
glass pieces that clink on the floor
like a Saturday morning cartoon character's.
Except he doesn't get back up.

And sometimes I am Yael.
I invite Hitler into my tent as he flees from his enemies.
He tells me he is thirsty, and I
give him milk, and he falls fast asleep.
I pick up a tent pin and hammer. I drive the pin
through his temple until it reaches the ground.

Other times I'm part of the plot to assassinate him
aboard his plane. This time I make sure
the bomb explodes. He falls faster and faster, crashing
with such force the earth swallows him up, as if he never

existed, and I'm sitting on the back porch, the sun is shining,
and all my grandparents, cousins, aunts, and uncles
are laughing and telling stories.

I V

Learning a New Language

My father is teaching me German.
He still speaks fluently, even though he
escaped from Nazi Germany almost
seventy years ago when he was seventeen.

We study nouns and verbs.
We study when to use the formal pronoun, *Sie*, you,
and when to use the more familiar, *Du*.
One must be offered permission to use the familiar.

We study dialects.
The word *Ich*, I.
The Berliners pronounce it *Ick*.
Those from Frankfurt am Main, *Isch*.
Those from Schwaben, *Ich* or *I*.

He tells me when he was a kid he and
his friends used to say in a Berliner dialect,
"*Berlin jeweesen Oranje jejessen und sie war so süss jeweesen.*"
I was in Berlin and ate an orange, and it was very sweet.
"And then we added, '*dass mir die brüh die gosh runterglaufe is,*'"
with the juices running down my mouth.
He explains: "It is in our Schwäbisch dialect.
I should say, it was our dialect."

Oma Kirchheimer

On Rechov Yafo in Jerusalem, people pack into buses,
and I watch mothers try to quiet their babies,
tell their older children to behave.

At Yad Vashem, I see pictures of people packed
into cattle cars and the mothers who tried to quiet their children.
I sit on a stone bench outside, try to get some air.

"I tried to get all my children out,
but it was too late.
There was nothing more I could do."

It's all right, Oma.
You did everything you could.
It's all right.
Don't go, I whisper.
But it's too late.

Sound Barrier

The screech is the shout of the children and grandchildren
of those whose ashes are at Auschwitz.
—Szewach Weiss, Israeli Ambassador to Poland

Three Israeli Air Force F-15s, invited by
the Polish government, thunder through overcast skies,

over Auschwitz, the screech breaking its silence.
Slowing, the jets follow the railroad tracks

leading into the camp, into the crematoria, then peel away.
Oma, Opa, Ruth, Josef, can you hear my screech

in every line, the breath of each stanza, the hiss
and moan of every poem?

You remain right behind my eyelids
as I write, letting each sound emerge,

primal and piercing, as I fly
on my own.

Ashes

Retired fire captain Bill Butler comes each day,
searching for his son,
      "Where are you, boy?"
each day, ten hours,
one hundred and eighteen days so far,
searching rubble that goes sixty feet below the earth
to bring his son home, to bury him.

Where I search, there is no rubble,
only different layers of ash, bits of scattered bone, broken stories,
      "Where are you, Oma,
near the barbed wire, in the ovens, the chimneys?"

Brian Lyons looks for his brother, a firefighter,
      "I know he's talking to me. 'Brian, don't quit. I'm in here.'"

Oma Kirchheimer came to me once, told me to stop looking,
"I'm not there any more. I've escaped
into the air, into particles so small they can no longer
be seen by the living."

Possessions

Mina Laub walked from Town Hall to the nearest phone
and called my father's mother, told her to send a heavy coat.

He put his hand in one pocket
of his winter coat and found his tefillin.

His siddur was in the other pocket.
He thought his mother had made him a sandwich.

He stood in line to strip, stood in line to turn
in his coat, his clothes, empty his pockets.

The Jehovah's Witnesses prisoners took
his belongings and put them in storage.

At his release, he got back his coat, his clothes,
his tefillin. Someone had stolen his siddur.

My father tells me he wants to be buried with his tefillin.

Maastricht, January, 2007

I am outside Wilhelmina Singel 88.
The skies are gray.
I take a deep breath and enter the building.
I walk up to the third floor. That's where you lived.
Before deportation.
Before Westerbork.
Before Auschwitz.
I knock on the door, hoping someone is there.
Hoping someone will let me in.
The door is locked.
I stay for a while.
I walk back down and sit on the curb across the street.
I stare up at the third floor.
I wonder what your life was like in 1942.
Did you stay at home most times, afraid to go out on the street,
the yellow star on your overcoats announcing
you wherever you went?
The synagogue you went to is still there.
There is a plaque to those deported from Maastricht to Westerbork,
then to Auschwitz or Sobibor. That's where most of you went.
Cars go by, people walk past, and I sit
watching the third floor, waiting for something to tell me it's time to go.
The street is beautiful, you know, tree-lined, well kept.
A light rain begins to fall.
Oma, Opa, Ruth, and Josef, you jump from the third floor. I catch you
and carry you to America with me.

Dogs

"I came across something," my father tells me
as I'm driving him to cardiac rehab, "in my mind,"
as if his mind were a filing cabinet
or the dish where coins and keys are kept.
It was something an old man told him when he was a boy,
how the stones freeze in winter, but the dogs
who chase you don't, and two days later we're sitting
on the back porch on Rosh Hashanah afternoon,
and he tells me that the way of life
he grew up with in southern Germany
no longer exists and if he thinks about it too much
it will make him crazy and is not worth
the consequences, and I want to tell him that I can hear
the cantor singing in shul, and I can smell the raisin challahs
his mother baked for a sweet New Year.
But it will not stop the dogs, so we just sit there
and watch the birds that have gathered at the feeder.

The Bird Feeder

He goes out on the back porch, makes sure
there is enough seed in the feeder, places

small pieces of bread on the railing and throws
some on the lawn for the ground feeders.

In the summer, he sits in his chair on the porch
and waits for the birds. In the winter,

he watches from his chair at the kitchen table.
Soon they come, white-throated, vesper,

and savannah sparrows, northern cardinals, slate-colored
juncos, black-capped chickadees, rusty blackbirds and

crows so big you could put a saddle on them and ride out.
Squirrels come too, hanging upside down

on the feeder trying to get the sunflower seeds,
leaving the millet and other grains.

Each March, he watches for the black-billed cuckoos
who bring the spring with them.

He calls the downy woodpecker Woody. Woody is his favorite, but
doesn't come very often. He says that's what makes him special.

One day he tells me how, when he was a boy in Germany,
before he fled in 1939, the swallows would come back each spring,

nesting in his family's barn where it was warm, flying
in and out looking for food for their young.

Now he feeds them all, delights in their colors and shapes,
at the way they eat and spit out the seeds.

Late in the afternoon, the sparrows fly off to sleep
in the forsythia bush. He sweeps the porch

as it turns to evening, sits in his chair, listening
to the crows perched on the roof call to one another.

Thinning Out the Carrots

It's July in New England,
and my father and I
are working in the garden,
thinning out the carrots.

"We got visas
for my mother and Josef
to get out of Germany in 1941
and go to Cuba. Instead

they went to Holland
to be with my father and sister,
who'd gone there in 1940, and waited
for their visas to America.
My mother said the family should stay together."

He puts his head down
and continues
thinning out the carrots.

Planting

Bringing the dirt to his face,
my father smells it. "This is good soil,"
Blessed are You,

and we plant the garden, and
my father tells me he dreamed

while in the hospital
of his garden, dreamed of it

all winter, and he made a vow,
a vow he'd plant again this year,
King of the universe, and

he tells me when planting seeds
stay in the middle of the row,

don't go too far to the left or too far to the right,
and each morning he goes to his garden,
who gives us life,

tends his plants the way he tends
his children, whispers "Grow,"

urges them to wrap their tendrils
around the fence, hang on,

and we water the plants, listen
to water as it drips, falls from leaf to leaf,

to the soil, and my father tells me
some days he can almost see the vegetables

growing in the sunlight, and I tell him
sometimes I can too,
sustains us and brings us to this time

and before eating the vegetables we make
the blessing for tasting food the first time in its season.

NOTES

Regarding two words that Rabbi Irving "Yitz" Greenberg uses in his Introduction to this book: The Shoah (Hebrew) is the Holocaust; Kaddish (Hebrew) is the memorial prayer recited for the dead.

■

Echoes (page 8): My father went to Berlin as part of the Youth Aliyah program founded by Henrietta Szold. Youth Aliyah worked to rescue German Jewish youth in the 1930s and send them to Israel (then Palestine). His stay in Berlin was also sponsored by the ORT program, an international movement dedicated to teaching young Jews the manual trades. My father was taught tool and die making. He also attended a yeshiva learning program operated by Mizrachi, a religious Zionist movement founded in 1902. Through any of these programs, he hoped to emigrate to Israel, but his visa came through for America first.

How I Knew and When (page 9): Israelitisch Meisjes Weeshuis (Dutch), Jewish girls' orphanage; *Juffrouw* (Dutch), Miss; *Tante* (German), aunt; *Onkel* (German), uncle. Juffrouw Rebecca Frank was killed in Sobibor.

Regarding Niederstetten, Shabbos Morning, March 25, 1933 (page 11): Shabbos (Hebrew), Sabbath; *Opa* (German), grandfather; *gendarme*, the French term for policeman, was used in the region where my father lived. Shul (German/Yiddish), synagogue. Pastor Umfrid is remembered with a plaque at Yad Vashem, the Memorial to the Holocaust in Israel, as a Righteous Gentile.

Summer Afternoon, 1934 (page 13): Max Kirchheimer and his wife, Zilli, were deported to Izbica in Poland on May 26, 1942, and were killed there.

Keeping Watch, 1936 (page 14): *Grossvater* (German), grandfather; Hitler Jugend (German), Hitler Youth; *shomer* (Hebrew), a watcher, a guard. Abraham Kirchheimer, my father's grandfather, got a visa to come to America in 1940, at the age of 85.

Traces (page 15): *shochet* (Hebrew), ritual slaughterer; *shacharis* (Hebrew), morning prayer service. The Nazi government law prohibiting the kosher slaughter of meat went into effect on December 7, 1933. My father said his family continued to have the *shochet* come until 1937, when it got too dangerous. Gerson Rosenthal and his wife, Rosa, volunteered to go on a deportation to Riga on December 1, 1941, with a widow and her three children so she and her children wouldn't have to go alone. The Rosenthals were killed in Riga, along with the widow and one of her children.

Berlin to Hamburg, Summer, 1938 (page 16): Brownshirts were *Sturmabteilung*, or *SA*, German stormtroopers. Tallis (Hebrew), ritual prayer shawl; tefillin (Hebrew), phylacteries. Therese Löwenthal taught in a Jewish girls' high school in Hamburg. She was deported to Riga on December 6, 1941. A man who survived Riga and knew my father told him that Therese taught children there. She, along with other Jews, was put on a truck one day in 1942 and taken out of Riga and then for some reason they were all brought back. The man said they were taken out late in the day, and he thinks that the men assigned to shoot the Jews went home. The next day, she was taken out of Riga again and did not return. Most Jews were taken to the nearby Rumbula Forest and shot.

Town Hall (page 17): *Trink* (German), drink.

Breaking Laws (page 18): a prisoner who worked in a concentration camp in a lower administrative position was called a kapo (origin uncertain, possibly Italian).

Lines (page 20): I obtained a copy of my father's entry in the Zugangs-Buch, Entrance Book, from Dachau, which is now housed in the National Archives and Records Administration in College Park, Maryland. The book was taken by the American Army when they liberated Dachau. My father's occupation is listed in it as *Schüler*, student. His number was 23344. His name is misspelled in the book as "Hirschheimer."

A Good Job (page 23): *Baracke* (German), barracks; *Stube* (German), room.

Shopping in Dachau (page 27): My father told me that the SS officers who ran the store were glad when prisoners came; they wanted to make money. The camp guards didn't bother prisoners at night if they knew the prisoners were going to the store.

Josef (page 33): *Guten Abend, Gute Nacht* (German), Good Evening, Good Night (Brahms' Lullaby; there are many variations on the lyrics); *Hamal'ach hago'el* (Hebrew), one of the prayers said at bedtime.

House of Cards (page 38): *Der Tag*, daily Yiddish paper sold in New York City.

The Photograph in My Hand (page 41): *Jude* (German), Jew.

Retelling (page 42): *Oma* (German), grandmother; Haggadoth (Hebrew), the books used at Passover that retell the Biblical story of the exodus of the Israelites from Egypt; Pesach (Hebrew), Passover.

My Mother's Sister, Resi (page 44): *Kindermädchen* (German), nanny. My mother's sister, Resi, was nineteen years older than my mother. She was unable to obtain a visa until 1939 and she came alone to America in November, 1939, sailing from Rotterdam.

This Is How My Opa Strauss Died (page 46): After my mother got her U.S. visa in Stuttgart in December, 1937, she went back to the orphanage in Amsterdam. In March, 1938, Oma and Opa Strauss went from Germany by train to Amsterdam to pick up my mother at the orphanage, and the three then went by train to Paris, took another train to Le Havre, and from there sailed to America.

Comforts (page 49): *kiddush, motzi* (Hebrew), the blessings said over wine and bread.

Brothers (page 51): My father's nickname, Bule (pronounced Booleh), is taken from the word *Bub* (German), boy. In his Schwäbisch dialect, a little boy is a *Bubele*, and that was shortened to Bule.

Tell Me, Josef (page 54): Joods Historisch Museum (Dutch), the Jewish Historical Museum in Amsterdam.

Found: Four Postcards to a Friend Before Deportation to Auschwitz (page 55): *Barak* (Dutch), barracks. Josef was learning Dutch while living in Maastricht, Holland. The postcards were written in the diction and grammar of a boy who was learning a new language, and contain German phrases as well.

Justice (page 63): "Putting a Price On the Holocaust? Not Even Close," by Clyde Haberman, *New York Times*, August 3, 2004.

Grand Central Station (page 75): Mengele was the Nazi doctor at Auschwitz who supervised selections of arriving transports, determining those to be killed and those sent to work. He also performed medical experiments on prisoners. His nickname was "the Angel of Death."

Rituals (page 84): mitzvah (Hebrew); commandment.

Some of the Things I Wonder (page 86): *Haarschnitt* (German), haircut; sukkah (Hebrew), a booth erected to commemorate the holiday of Sukkot.

Sweet Dreams (page 89): Yael kills Sisera in this manner in Chapter 4 of the Book of Judges.

Learning a New Language (page 93): "Those from Schwaben, *Ich* or *I*." This *I* is pronounced "ee." The Berliner dialect is written as standard German but is pronounced as I have transliterated it. The Schwäbisch dialect is spelled and pronounced differently from standard German.

Oma Kirchheimer (page 94): Rechov Yafo (Hebrew), Jaffa Street. Yad Vashem (Hebrew), "a memorial and a name," is taken from the Book of Isaiah, 56:5: "And to them I will give in my house and within my walls a memorial and a name … that shall not be cut off."

Possessions (page 97): siddur (Hebrew), prayer book.

ACKNOWLEDGMENTS

To Mary Stewart Hammond, without whom there would be no book. An extraordinary poet and generous teacher and mentor, she has nurtured my belief in this work, and her teaching is reflected throughout this book. I am forever grateful.

Special thanks to the poets in Mary Stewart Hammond's master class, for their inspiration and helpful feedback. They have enriched my poetry and my life.

To Elizabeth Macklin, whose kindness, insights, and advice have been invaluable.

To Rabbi Hayyim Angel, Rabbi Yitzchak Berger, Ruth Bregman, Han-Hua Chang, Katie Cronan-Sawert, Sally Lipton Derringer, Karen Frankl, Israel Fridman, Lisa Korman Goldenberg, Lois Gottesman, Michael Gottsegen, Ph.D., Blu Greenberg, Rabbi Irving "Yitz" Greenberg, Sandy Gross, Paul Lardinois and family, Ruth and Del Mileski, Margot Mindich, Nina Moinester, Rabbi Walter Orenstein, Jaclyn Piudik, Minnie Bruce Pratt, Elinor Roden, and Raquel Solomon. Their encouragement, guidance, and friendship have made all the difference.

To the faculty and staff at CLAL–The National Jewish Center for Learning and Leadership—Meredith Appell, Rabbi Tsvi Blanchard, Dale Brown, Judy Epstein, Rabbi Steven Greenberg, Rabbi Brad Hirschfield, Rabbi David Kalb, Theresa Perruzza, Anna Rakhlin, and Cynthia Schupf—whose belief in my work has meant so much to me. To Aliza J. Kaplan, for her expert designer's eye. Especially to Rabbi Irwin Kula and Donna M. Rosenthal, whose infinitely generous trust and support have made my dream come true. Thank you.

To the editors of the following publications in which poems in this book have appeared, some in slightly different versions: *CrossCurrents*, *Heart*, *Jewish Women's Literary Annual*, *Kalliope*, *Lilith*, *Mima'amakim*, *The Mother in Our Lives*, *Nashim*, *Natural Bridge*, *Poetica*, *Poetry NZ*, *Potomac Review*, and *Sambatyon*. Also to the editors of *beliefnet.com*, *Jewish Family and Life.com*, and *MSN Religion Forum* websites, where poems have appeared.

Photographs and documents: Personal collection; Joods Historisch Museum, Amsterdam; and National Archives and Records Administration, College Park, Maryland.

ABOUT THE AUTHOR

Janet R. Kirchheimer's work has appeared in publications such as *Alimentum*, *Atlanta Review*, *Kalliope*, *Lilith*, *Natural Bridge*, *Poetry NZ*, and *Potomac Review*. Her essay "Make Your Selection, Please" was a JTA Feature article for Yom Hashoah. In 2006-07, she was a Drisha Institute for Jewish Education Arts Fellow. She is Assistant to the President/Director of Community Development at CLAL–The National Jewish Center for Learning and Leadership, and teaches adults and teens about Judaism in a variety of locations using poetry and creative-writing exercises. She also leads a monthly "Poetry Shmooze" at the Spanish and Portuguese Synagogue in New York City, where she lives.

ABOUT CLAL

CLAL–The National Jewish Center for Learning and Leadership stimulates volunteer, professional and rabbinic leadership to build responsive Jewish communities across America; helps individuals imagine new Jewish possibilities; promotes inclusive Jewish communities in which all voices are heard; develops insights from Jewish wisdom for the American public square; and enhances Jewish participation in American civic and spiritual life.

The CLAL faculty, representing rabbis and scholars from a variety of streams and disciplines, imbues young and established leaders with skills and training for building dynamic Jewish communities. Since CLAL was founded in 1974, it has earned a reputation for excellence, creating compelling programs and resources that embody the principles of openness and diversity. CLAL's unique, creative approach combines Jewish intellectual traditions with innovative scholarship to transform American Jewish life. Virtually every Jewish community in America has been touched by CLAL.

Among its initiatives, CLAL is recognized for helping Americans in the 1970's begin to face and address the Holocaust, and for its significant role in the creation of the United States Holocaust Memorial Council and Museum.

Today, CLAL is proud to publish this emotionally powerful and eloquent book of poetry which gives a new voice to the Holocaust and its impact on our lives.

CLAL

440 Park Avenue South, 4th Floor
New York, NY 10016
(212)779-3300 Fax: (212)779-1009
www.clal.org